CU00693394

WHAT TEENAGERS SAY... AND WHAT THEY REALLY MEAN!

She's a GOAT!

It's A NOOB

A HILARIOUS GUIDE TO HELP YOU WORK OUT WHAT ON EARTH YOUR TEENAGER IS GOING ON ABOUT

BB

books by
BOXER

www.booksbyboxer.com

Published in the UK by
Books By Boxer, Leeds, LS13 4BS
© Books By Boxer 2016
All Rights Reserved

ISBN: 9781909732520

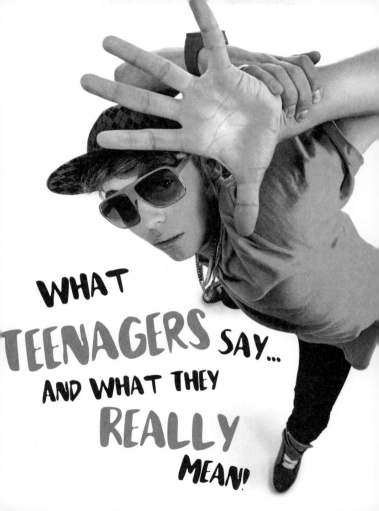

WHAT
TEENAGERS SAY...
AND WHAT THEY
REALLY
MEAN!

If your kids have hit the teen years and you're wondering what they really are getting up to when they stay they are 'studying at their friends on a Friday night'. This handy little guide will help you decipher the REAL meaning behind what they tell you!

Teenage years are when nature tells you to move on.

It's a bit like a bird's nest. When the chicks are young they get food, warmth, security, a home provided by parent birds, acting out of natural instincts to protect and nurture their young. So why would these young birds ever want to leave?

Because, at a certain age, nature dictates that they should leave, to find a mate and build their own nest as a continuation of the species, and it does this through hormones. These hormones set the restless genes in motion with subliminal suggestions of discontent, such as, get a mate, get better food, build your own nest, build your own life.

Teenagers are like these young birds.

Although they probably don't know it, they are being prepared to flee the nest!

Rebelliousness, gloom, surliness, dissatisfaction with home life is all part of 'breaking out of the nest' and it's perfectly natural and easy to understand once you know what's going on.

Teen-speak is just another component of this 'pre-exodus'.

Teenage language evolves with each generation. Teenagers need to be different.

However cool and hip parents think it is to identify with teenage culture, music, dress, language, teenagers don't want to be understood by the older generation, so they develop words that they hope only their peer group (the squad) can understand.

Many new, cool words, signs and phrases come from music and music videos, hip hop and rapping being a popular source.

However, kids make up their own words and if it catches with the squad (your group of friends) then it could be 'lit', 'high-key' or 'live' (cool, exciting, fun).

So stay 'woke' dudes and get down with the kids!

The Real Meanings Of The Word "Whatever"

A favourite of the common or garden teenager, the word 'whatever' is the cause of frustration in many a family discussion. Following are possible meanings of this oft-used phrase...

What the teenager says

Whatever

What this really means

I disagree, but I can't be arsed to argue with you.

What the teenager says

Whatever

What this really means

I know you're right but I won't admit it.

Whatever

What this really means

You're an adult, so you're probably right.

What the teenager says

Whatever

What this really means

I'm not really bothered.

What the teenager says

Whatever

What this really means

I'm so not listening to you.

what the teenager says

Whatever

What this really means

Yeh, right.

What the teenager says

Whatever

What this really means

I think you're confusing me with someone who gives an actual shit.

What the teenager says

Whatever

What this really means

I've lost the argument or I know I'm not going to get my own way, so this makes it looks like I don't care.

The Meaning Of "Silence"

Silence can mean lot's of things and you should exercise caution around a teenager when they are in silent mode.

What the teenager says

[Silence]

What this really means

I'm a brooding, foreboding teenager.

What the teenager says

[Silence]

What this really means

I have exhausted my patience with you.

What the teenager says

[Silence]

What this really means

I'm in a mood.

What the teenager says

[Silence]

What this really means

I am giving the appearance of being deeper than I actually am.

General Teenage Speak

Although it may initially seem that teenagers communicate through a series of simple grunts and moans, their language and 'speak' can be complicated. What you think may be a perfectly reasonable response to these simple grunts and moans can evoke wrath like hell has exploded!

What the teenager says

I cleaned my room.

What this really means

I cleared a path from the bed to the door.

What the teenager says

Can I have a couple of friends over?

What this really means

My friends are here... ten of them, and more are on the way.

What the teenager says

I can't.

What this really means

I won't.

What the teenager says

You wouldn't understand.

What this really means

No one could possibly understand. My current problem is actually the biggest problem in the world.

We're just frenemies.

What this really means

This particular friend is OK to hang out with but can't be trusted, unlike a real friend, not to say things behind your back. He or She is someone who puts you down occasionally and can't be relied upon.

what the teenager says

I'll do it later.

What this really means

I won't... unless you are going to apply force, blackmail, withdrawal of privileges, money or other things I need. Otherwise, NOPE!

What the teenager says

FML
(F*ck My Life)

What this really means

I'm not happy with the current situation.

What this really means

Not literally, figuratively.

Example: "We are literally killing ourselves laughing"

YOLO
(You Only Live Once)

What this really means

I'm about to do something stupid/ illegal/ immoral.

What the teenager says

Do you like this selfie?

What this really means

Am I gorgeous?

what the teenager says

LOL
(Laugh Out Loud)

What this really means

Wasn't funny, but at least I've responded.

What the teenager says

I need a job.

What this really means

I need money, preferably not by working!

What the teenager says

I've literally got nothing to wear.

What this really means

All my clothes are on my bedroom floor.

What the teenager says

There's nothing to eat.

What this really means

There's nothing to eat that can be microwaved in less than 3 minutes.

I know that.

What this really means

I don't know that, but that's what Google is for.

I still know more things than most people, especially the older generation who weren't very well educated. They didn't even have phones and computers back then so how did they manage to learn anything... go to the library?!?

What the teenager says

She's a face jerk.

What this really means

She's a Facebook addict.

What the teenager says

Her hair is on fleek.

What this really means

Her hair is so cool.

Her hair is on fire.

What this really means

Her hair is not cool.

What the teenager says

These are my party sludge rides.

What this really means

These trainers used to be white.

What the teenager says

We were killing it last night.

What this really means

They stood around, scared to talk to girls, talking about Call of Duty.

What the teenager says

It was good to chat.

What this really means

I'm blocking you.

What the teenager says

I wasn't staring.

What this really means

They caught me glaring.

What the teenager says

I can't even...
(While shaking head)

What this really means

Speechless.

What the teenager says

Yeh, she's an EMO but she's one of my mains.

What this really means

She's my cousin and I've been told I have to be friends with the morbid, boring, goth-like drama queen.

I'm feeling cashed but tonight I'm turning up and gonna get merked and turnt.

What this really means

Although I'm tired, tonight I'm gonna pump myself up and go out and get myself drunk, high and crazy!

what the teenager says

Now my Mum is chirping about my ship but in the end it's NBD.

What this really means

My Mum is giving me grief about my relationship but it's no big deal.

What the teenager says

I was just about
to do that.

What this really means

I have no intention of doing
that and I don't even know
why you bothered asking me

What the teenager says

Their parents are really cool.

What this really means

Their parents let them do the things you won't let me do. So I'm going to make you jealous until you do.

What the teenager says

I am listening to you!

What this really means

I have no idea what you just said.

What the teenager says

Everybody else
is doing it.

What this really means

No one is actually doing
it, but I'm going to try and
make you feel really bad that
you're not letting me do it.

What the teenager says

SMH

What this really means

Acronym for *"shake my head"*.

It's what teens will say about you if you use their slang. ie "Woman just said my outfit was on fleek. SMH".

What the teenager says

It was good to chat but I never give out my ASL.
(Age, Sex, Location)

What this really means

We've seen each other but we're no way into DTR yet.
(Defining the relationship)

What the teenager says

He/she is a GOAT

What this really means

Acronym for
Greatest Of All Time

What the teenager says

He's a N00B, down for EPICFAIL in life.

What this really means

He's no interest in learning, a loser and is bound to come unstuck.

What the teenager says

Netflix and Chill

What this really means

Netflix and chill has nothing to do with watching movies or relaxing but everything to do with hooking up.

What the teenager says

How does she get so crunk on so little cheddar?

What this really means

How does she get so drunk on so little money?

LMIRL

What this really means

Acronym for
Let's Meet In Real Life.

What the teenager says

CU46

What this really means

Acronym for
See you for sex.

What the teenager says

CUL8TR46

What this really means

See you later for sex.

What the teenager says

MOS/DOS/POS

What this really means

Mum/ Dad/ Parent Over Shoulder. This alerts the person you are talking to not to send anything that's not PEP (Parent Eye Positive).

What the teenager says

You don't understand.

What this really means

Nobody could understand my complicated world, especially you who has never lived through any of this. (Parents: trying to explain you HAVE lived through all of this is a waste of time)

What the teenager says

Leave me alone.

What this really means

I know this sounds bad but I just need some space. I hope I'll be forgiven for that outburst. (Parents: this sounds much worse than it really is... don't overreact)

I'm bored.

What this really means

I'm annoyed, stressed out for no good reason, probably hormones. It's all so boring, an alien could walk in through the front door and would just be basic. Nothing, repeat nothing, could possibly interest me right now...

...apart from the current girl / guy of my dreams suddenly appearing from nowhere!

What the teenager says

Yes, my friends are great.

What this really means

I can't really talk about this but I should really talk about it because it's so confusing! My friends ARE great and I want to be just like them but also I want to stand out and be different to them. Is that normal?

What the teenager says

Yes, of course he/she is ok!

What this really means

You may not approve of my friend, and you may be right, but I have to figure this one out for myself.

What the teenager says

My friend's got a tattoo.

What this really means

I've no intention of getting a tattoo...
YET!

But my parents have been getting on my
nerves a bit lately and this will guarantee
to send them through the roof.

What the teenager says

I *do* want you to meet my friends.

What this really means

I can't let you meet them!

I suffer from 'role friction' and my personality is different with friends and parents!
When I'm with my parents I think I'm my normal self but when my friends and my family are together I hardly dare speak for fear of appearing ridiculous to either of them.

What the teenager says

Why are you being so emotional?
It's so immature.
It's so immature.

What this really means

I'm deflecting the telling off
I was getting!

I shouldn't really but it puts Mum
on the backfoot so well!
(Parents: don't fall for this. Being emotional
is NOT immature. You're emotional
because you care.)

What the teenager says

I hate you.

What this really means

I'm really angry, I'm impulsive and I'm not good at expressing myself.

Of course I don't mean it but I've said it now so I will ride it out and hope that I haven't blown it. (Parents: this is the 'biggie' we all dread but it is usually a knee jerk reaction to a pent up situation. Most teenagers will be remorseful after they have calmed down. Tell them how hurtful it was and they might think twice about saying it again. Don't overreact.)

What the teenager says

I'm so over it.

What this really means

I still care but don't
want you to know that.

What parents say to teens...

and what they really mean!

And some nice things to say to your teenager!

What the parent says

It's not as if I
don't trust you.

What this really means

I don't trust you.

What the parent says

Your body is changing
and you have to adapt
to this change.

What this really means

I have to adapt
to this change.

What the parent says

Your hormones
are raging.

What this really means

And this scares the crap
out of me.

Don't grow up so fast.

What this really means

Don't have sex.

What the parent says

Be responsible.

What this really means

Don't get pregnant!

What the parent says

Be home before 11pm.

What this really means

I'll start panicking when it gets to 2.00am.

What the parent says

Be proud of yourself and
what you are doing.

What this really means

Sometimes you just put
yourself down too much.

What the parent says

It doesn't matter what results you get as long as you work hard and do your best. But you are special and will always do well.

What this really means

It DOES matter what results you get but I would rather have lower grades than a screwed up teenager. He/she is special and will always do well, but I suppose every parent thinks that.

What the parent says

I worry when you're out but I know you will do things right because you are smart.

What this really means

Hopefully this ill placed trust will make them more responsible.

What the parent says

Always be well turned out and be confident, even if you don't feel it.

What this really means

This is what my mum said to me and though I thought it was stupid at the time it actually works.

I worry about you,
but I trust you.

What this really means

Trust is a very powerful
two-way thing. I give mine
and hopefully he/she will
return that trust.

What the parent says

Nice hair, good shoes and punctuality will get you half of the way there. The rest is up to you.

What this really means

It works for me.

What the parent says

I want to know where you are going, who with and what time you'll be coming home... because I care.

What this really means

Because I care... but also I don't want you to make all the mistakes that I made at your age!

What the parent says

I'll always be there
for you, whatever
happens in your life.

What this really means

mean that right now but it's a
two-way thing and don't give
me any reason in the future not
to keep this promise

TEEN-SPEAK IS BAE

(Basically Always Excellent)

Teenagers are fundamentally children in fairly grown up bodies and though they can give the impression, in some cases, of being surly, negative, incommunicative awkward, uncooperative, untidy, rebellious and lazy, they have the same vulnerabilities and sensitivities as younger children, – an ill judged remark could bring many of them close to tears.

They can also be quite lovable and generally speaking, BAE.

They may often be bad but mostly they don't mean it.

Having a language of their own that only friends and other members of the teenage world can understand is quite useful in sharing knowledge, dealing with the traumas of teenage life and learning helpful hints on how to gain the precious freedoms from well meaning but occasionally over protective parents.

So, just like the young birds in the nest, the 'lesser spotted teenagers' (and the spotted ones) have a lot to learn before they gain their freedom and fly away.

So if the sound of tweeting can be heard late at night it might just be your 'little birds', communicating with their fledgling friends on social media, making preparations for the best way to fly, and flee the nest.